# 롤러코스터
## 이래서 강력추천합니다!

**체계적인 학습** | 초등학교 교육 과정을 충실히 반영하고 교과서 지문을 최대한 활용함으로써 학생들이 배워야 할 주요 학습 내용을 체계적으로 익힐 수 있도록 하였습니다.

**학년별 맞춤 학습** | 모든 학년에서 표현과 낱말 학습을 기본으로 하되, 1·2학년은 Phonics, 3·4학년은 Reading & Writing, 5·6학년은 Grammar를 다루는 등, 각 학년별 주요 학습 영역을 중점적으로 다룸으로써 학년별 맞춤 학습을 추구하였습니다.

**균형적인 학습** | 읽기, 쓰기 학습뿐만 아니라 오디오 CD와 동영상 CD를 활용한 듣기, 말하기 학습을 통해 영어의 4개 영역(Listening, Speaking, Reading, Writing)을 고루 마스터할 수 있도록 하였습니다.

**자발적인 학습** | Song, Chant를 통해 표현을 자연스럽게 익히고, Cartoon을 통해 배운 내용을 재미있게 정리 하는 등 다양한 Activity를 통해 학생들이 흥미를 가지고 적극적으로 수업에 참여할 수 있도록 하였습니다.

**동영상을 통한 원어민과의 학습** | 원어민의 발음과 입모양을 동영상 CD를 통해 정확히 인지하고 학습자의 발음을 녹음해 원어민의 발음과 비교하여 들어 보게 함으로써 학습자 스스로 발음을 교정할 수 있는 기회를 제공 하였습니다.

# Roller coaster

## set 구성

# 01 Student Book_ Unit 1, 3

## Conversation

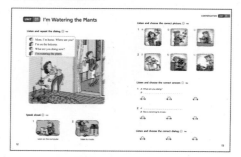

초등영어 교과과정과 연계된 표현을 학습하고, 다양한 활동을 통해 표현을 익혀 봐요.

## Words

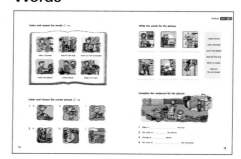

생활 영어 표현과 관련된 낱말을 학습하고, 재미있게 낱말을 익혀 봐요.

## Reading

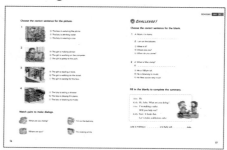

표현에 대한 이해력을 높이고, 각종 경시대회 및 TOFEL iBT에 대비할 수 있는 문제를 풀어 봐요.

## Writing

학습한 표현을 써 보면서, 자유롭게 활용할 수 있는 능력을 키워 봐요.

## Cartoon

재미있는 만화를 통해 이미 학습한 표현과 낱말을 종합 정리해 봐요.

## Test

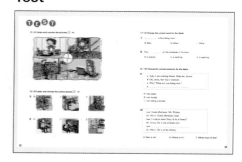

테스트를 통해 학습한 표현 및 낱말에 대한 학습 성취도를 점검해 봐요.

# Student Book _ Unit 2, 4

## Cartoon

재미있는 만화를 통해 앞으로 배울 핵심 문법
사항을 미리 알아봐요.

## Grammar point 1

핵심 문법 사항을 익히고 다양한 활동을 통해
응용해 봐요.

## Grammar point 2

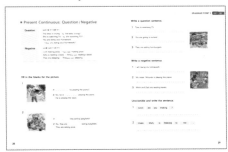

핵심 문법 사항을 익히고 다양한 활동을 통해
응용해 봐요.

## Story

학습한 문법을 활용한 흥미로운 이야기를 읽고
문제를 풀어 봐요.

## Story words

이야기에서 학습한 낱말을 예문을 통해
종합 정리해 봐요.

## Test

테스트를 통해 학습한 문법에 대한 이해도와
응용력을 평가해 봐요.

# 02 Workbook

낱말을 따라 쓴 다음, 우리말에 해당하는
낱말을 직접 써 봐요.

표현을 따라 쓴 다음, 우리말에 해당하는
표현을 직접 써 봐요.

잘 듣고, 빈칸에 알맞은 낱말과
표현을 자신있게 써 봐요.

# 03 권말 테스트

낱말 및 표현에 관한 문제를 풀면서 그동안 쌓은
실력을 마음껏 발휘해 봐요.
(Achievement Test / Final Test)

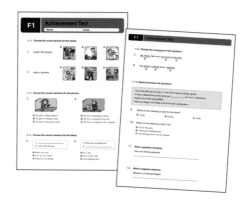

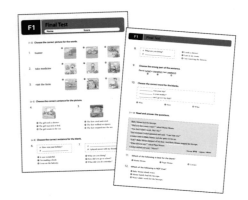

# 04 동영상 CD

## Conversation

초등영어 교과과정과 연계된 표현을 배워 봐요.

## Words

생활영어 표현과 관련된 낱말을 배워 봐요.

## Speak

학습한 낱말들을 녹음해 원어민의 발음과
비교해 봐요.

# 05 오디오 CD

Student Book, Workbook의 내용과 노래 및
챈트가 담겨 있어요.

# Learning Points

## F1

| Unit Title | Theme | Function (Unit 1&3)<br>Grammar (Unit 2&4) | Conversation (Unit 1&3)<br>Language Item (Unit 2&4) |
|---|---|---|---|
| **1**<br>I'm Watering the Plants | Present Continuous | · Talking about what one is doing | Mom, I'm home. Where are you?<br>I'm on the balcony.<br>What are you doing now?<br>I'm watering the plants. |
| **2**<br>What Is Alice Doing? | Present Continuous | · Present continuous:<br>how to make -ing form,<br>making question,<br>negative sentences | I am going to school.<br>She is not playing the piano.<br>Are they drawing pictures? |
| **3**<br>How Was Your Vacation? | Past Simple | · Expressing experiences of past using past simple | How was your vacation?<br>It was great. I had a great time.<br>What did you do during your vacation?<br>I took a trip to Hawaii with my family. |
| **4**<br>I Went to the Cinema | How / What<br>Past Simple | · Question words:<br>how / what<br>· Past simple of verbs:<br>Regular and irregular verbs | How did you get to the library?<br>What did you do in London?<br>Jenny visited her cousin yesterday.<br>I swam in the sea with my brother. |

# F2

| Unit Title | Theme | Function (Unit 1&3)<br>Grammar (Unit 2&4) | Conversation (Unit 1&3)<br>Language Item (Unit 2&4) |
|---|---|---|---|
| ❶ I Have a Cold | Sickness<br>Cause & Result | · Expressing one's sickness | Are you OK? You look sick.<br>I have a cold.<br>Why are you so busy?<br>Because I have to finish this work. |
| ❷ Why Is the Alien in Our Garden? | Cause & Result | · Question 'why'<br>· Conjunction 'because' | Why are you so happy?<br>Because I got a present.<br>I don't eat pizza because I'm on a diet. |
| ❸ Would You Like to Come? | Suggestion | · Suggestion | Would you like to come to my house?<br>Yes, I'd love to.<br>Come to my house by 5 o'clock.<br>Okay. See you then. |
| ❹ Would You Help Me, Please? | Would | · Would like to<br>· Modal verb 'would' | Would you help me, please?<br>Would you like to try this pie?<br>I would like to loot at the menu. |

# F3

| Unit Title | Theme | Function (Unit 1&3)<br>Grammar (Unit 2&4) | Conversation (Unit 1&3)<br>Language Item (Unit 2&4) |
|---|---|---|---|
| ❶ Turn Off the TV | Commands | · Commands<br>· Negative commands | Turn off the TV.<br>Don't take off your shoes. |
| ❷ Don't Turn on the TV | Verb Phrases | · Commands<br>· Negative commands | Turn off the TV.<br>Don't turn off the TV. |
| ❸ I'm Going to Visit My Uncle Tomorrow | Future Tense with 'be going to' | · Describing what someone is doing | I'm going to visit my uncle tomorrow.<br>Are you going to go to the market tomorrow? |
| ❹ Are You Going to Go to the Namsan Tower? | Future Tense with 'be going to' | · Future tense with 'be going to' | I'm going to leave for Seoul tonight.<br>Are you going to go to the Namsan tower? |

# F4

| Unit Title | Theme | Function (Unit 1&3) Grammar (Unit 2&4) | Conversation (Unit 1&3) Language Item (Unit 2&4) |
|---|---|---|---|
| ❶ He Is Taller than Me | Comparative | · Comparing people and things | He is taller than me. The lion is stronger than the monkey. The train is faster than the car. |
| ❷ Mina Is Prettier than Me | Comparative | · The comparative | My father is older than my mother. Mina is prettier than me. What is stronger than monkey? |
| ❸ Sam Is the Tallest in My Class | Superlative | · Expressing the superlative | Are you taller than Sam? No, I'm not. Sam is the tallest in my class. |
| ❹ What Is the Smallest Animal? | Superlative | · The superlative | Jennifer is the smartest in her class. Today is the happiest day of my life. Who is the oldest in your family? |

# F5

| Unit Title | Theme | Function (Unit 1&3) Grammar (Unit 2&4) | Conversation (Unit 1&3) Language Item (Unit 2&4) |
|---|---|---|---|
| ❶ I Usually Clean My Room | Frequency Adverb | · Explaining frequency | How often do you clean your room? I help my mom on Mondays, Wednesdays and Fridays. I usually clean my room. |
| ❷ He Seldom Cooks | Frequency Adverb | · Frequency adverbs | How often does your father cook? He seldom cooks. |
| ❸ They're My Socks | Possessions | · Talking about possessions | Whose socks are they? They're my socks. They're mine. |
| ❹ Whose Dog Is That? | Whose & Possessions | · Question 'whose' · The possessive case and possessive pronoun | Whose dog is that? That is my dog. The dog is mine. |

# F6

| Unit Title | Theme | Function (Unit 1&3) Grammar (Unit 2&4) | Conversation (Unit 1&3) Language Item (Unit 2&4) |
|---|---|---|---|
| ❶ I Go to the Department Store by Car | Transportation | · Expressing means of transportation and time | How do you go to the department store? I go to the department store by car. How long does it take? It takes about 10 minutes. |
| ❷ How Long Does It Take? | How | · Question 'how' | How do you go to the store? How often do you wash your hair? How long does it take? How much are the sunglasses? |
| ❸ I Like Spring Better | Preference | · Talking about one's preference | Which season do you like better, spring or fall? I like spring better. |
| ❹ Which Do You Want, Soda or Juice? | Conjunction 'or' | · Conjunction 'or' | He is going to buy pants or shorts. Which do you want, soda or juice? |

Roller Coaster
# Contents

# UNIT 01   I Have a Cold

**Listen and repeat the dialog.** 🔘 T02

 Tina, are you OK? You look sick.

 I have a cold.

 Then why are you so busy?

 Because I have to finish this math homework.

 Oh, my! You should take a rest.

**Speak aloud.** 🔘 T03

**1**

have an earache

**2**

have a toothache

**3**

have a headache

12

## Listen and choose the correct picture. T04

1  ⓐ     ⓑ     ⓒ

2  ⓐ     ⓑ     ⓒ

## Listen and choose the correct answer. T05

1  *A:* Are you OK? You look sick.

   *B:* _____

2  *A:* _____

   *B:* Because I have to finish this math homework.

## Listen and choose the correct dialog. T06

## Listen and repeat the words. T07

have a toothache

have a headache

have a stomachache

have an earache

have a backache

have a cold

## Listen and choose the correct sentence for the picture. T08

1

ⓐ   ⓑ

2

ⓐ   ⓑ

**Write the word for the picture.**

| stomachache | earache | headache | backache |
|---|---|---|---|

1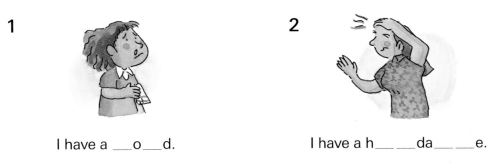

_____

2

_____

3

_____

4

_____

**Fill in the blanks.**

1

I have a __ o __ d.

2

I have a h__ __ da__ __ e.

3

I have a __ __ oma__ __ a__ __ e.

4

I have a too__ __ ache.

**Who's who?**

Brian      Wendy      Tony      Julia

**1** I'm short. I have brown hair. I have a stomachache. Who am I? _____

**2** I'm tall. I have dark hair. I have a headache. Who am I? _____

**3** I'm short. I have brown hair. I have a backache. Who am I? _____

**4** I'm tall. I have dark hair. I have an earache. Who am I? _____

## Match the pairs to make a dialog.

**1**
| Are you OK? You look sick. | | Because I have to finish this work. |

**2**
| Why are you so busy? | | I have a toothache. |

 **CHALLENGE!**

**Choose the correct sentence for the blank.**

**1** *A:* _____

*B:* Because I have to finish my homework.

ⓐ Are you OK?

ⓑ What are you doing?

ⓒ Why are you so busy?


**2** *A:* Are you OK? You look sick.

*B:* _____

ⓐ I'm working.

ⓑ I'm very busy.

ⓒ I have an earache.


**Fill in the blanks to complete the summary.**

*Julie:* What are you doing?

*Andy:* I'm doing my homework.

*Julie:* Why didn't you do it yesterday?

*Andy:* Because I had a headache yesterday.

_____ didn't do his homework yesterday
because he had a _____ .

**What are they saying? Write.**

1 _____

2 _____

3 _____

4 _____

| | |
|---|---|
| I have a stomachache. | I have a backache. |
| I have a headache. | I have an earache. |

**Write the correct answer for the picture.**

Are you OK? You look sick.

_____

**Write the sentence for the picture and you can make a dialog.**

1    2    3    4    5

1    *John, are you OK? You look sick.*

2    _____

3    _____

4    _____

5    _____

Oh, my! You should take a rest.        John, are you OK? You look sick.

Then why are you so busy?              I have a headache.

Because I have to finish this math homework.


**Unscramble the words and write the sentence.**

1    | are you | why | so busy | ? |

    _____


2    | my homework | I | have to finish | because | . |

    _____

# I Have a **Headache**

머리가 아파요

**Choose and complete the cartoon.**

Go to bed.

I have a headache.

Why are you so busy?

I didn't finish my homework.

21

**[1~5]** Listen and number the picture. ○ T09

_____        _____        _____        _____        _____

**[6~7]** Listen and choose the correct dialog for the picture. ○ T10

**6**

ⓐ        ⓑ        ⓒ

**7**

ⓐ        ⓑ        ⓒ

[8~10] Write the correct letter for each sentence.

8 _____ I have an earache.

9 _____ I have a toothache.

10 _____ I have a stomachache.

ⓐ    ⓑ    ⓒ

[11~12] Choose the correct answer for the blank.

11

*Annie:* _____

*Joann:* Because I have many things to do.

*Annie:* Like what?

*Joann:* I have math homework, English homework, and science homework.

ⓐ Why is he late?            ⓑ Where are you going?

ⓒ Why are you so busy?

12

*Mike:* Why is Sam not here?

*Sonya:* Because he has a bad cold.

*Mike:* Oh, too bad. He can't go to the party.

Sam cannot go to the party _____.

ⓐ because he is not here            ⓑ because he is sick

ⓒ because he is too bad

# UNIT 02 Why Is the Alien in Our Garden?

**Quiz** | Q: _____ is the alien in the garden?

A: Maybe it wants to be the girls' friend.

**Quiz**

Q: Why did the boy come to the girls' house?

A: _____ he wants to scare them.

# ■ Question Word: Why

| Why + be동사 + 주어~? | Why are you busy?  왜 너는 바쁘니?<br>Why was Tom sad?  왜 탐은 슬펐니?<br>Why weren't Ron and Cindy in the party?<br>왜 론과 신디는 파티에 없었니? |
|---|---|
| Why + do [did] + 주어<br>+ 일반동사~? | Why do you want pizza?  왜 피자가 먹고 싶니?<br>Why did I go there?      왜 내가 거기에 갔을까?<br>Why didn't you write a letter to Sam?<br>왜 샘에게 편지를 쓰지 않았니? |
| Why + 조동사 + 주어<br>+ 일반동사~? | Why can't Ann go with us?     왜 앤은 우리와 함께 못 가니?<br>Why must I open the window?  왜 내가 창문을 열어야 하지? |

## Fill in the blank and complete the dialog.

**1**

A: _____ are you so happy?

B: Because I got a present.

**2**

A: _____ can't you play soccer?

B: Because I'm busy.

**3**

A: _____ did Eric make a cake?

B: Because it's his mom's birthday.

**4**

A: _____ doesn't Sue want a doll?

B: Because she has many dolls.

## Rewrite the sentence in the correct order.

**1** Are why they so excited?

_____

**2** Why you didn't study hard yesterday?

_____

**3** She wasn't why happy about the party?

_____

## Unscramble and complete the dialog.

**1** | are | why | you | late | ? |

A: _____

B: Because I slept late.

**2** | all wet | why | you | are | ? |

A: _____

B: Because I didn't have an umbrella with me.

**3** | that jacket | why | buy | did | Jake | ? |

A: _____

B: Because he likes the color.

**4** | Kim | was | why | so sad | ? |

A: _____

B: Because she failed the test.

# ■ Conjunction: Because

Tom joined the sports club. 톰은 스포츠 클럽에 가입했다.
He likes to play sports. 그는 운동하는 것을 좋아한다.

→ <u>Tom joined the sports club</u> because <u>he likes to play sports</u>.
　　　　　result　　　　　　　　　　　　　　cause

톰은 운동하는 것을 좋아하기 때문에 스포츠 클럽에 가입했다.

A: Why is Lucy so noisy? 루시는 왜 저렇게 소란을 피우니?
B: Because she is so hungry. 왜냐하면 굉장히 배가 고프기 때문이야.

## Fill in the blank and choose the correct picture.

**1** Jasmine came home early _____ she was sick.

ⓐ 　　　　ⓑ

**2** A: Why didn't you go on a picnic with your family?

　　B: _____ I had a test yesterday.

ⓐ 　　　　ⓑ

**Make a sentence using 'because'.**

**1** I don't eat pizza. I'm on a diet.

_____

**2** I didn't hear the noise. I fell asleep.

_____

**3** I'm cooking dinner. I want to surprise my parents.

_____


**Unscramble and write the sentence.**

**1** | walk the dog | he | because | had to | . |

A: Why did Tim go out?
B: _____

**2** | didn't | because | clean | we | after the party | . |

A: Why is it so dirty here?
B: _____

**3** | my bag | I | because | need | a new bag | is old | . |

_____

**4** | Sandy | because | she | sleepy | took a long nap | isn't | . |

_____

# The Ghost in the Campsite 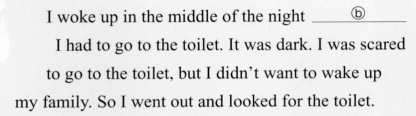 T11

A few months ago, my family had a trip to Canada. Dad drove very long hours. It was getting dark, so we found a campsite and set up the tent. We had dinner together and then tried to sleep. We had to sleep early _____ⓐ_____ we had to leave early in the morning.

I woke up in the middle of the night _____ⓑ_____ I had to go to the toilet. It was dark. I was scared to go to the toilet, but I didn't want to wake up my family. So I went out and looked for the toilet. I wasn't so scared because the light was on. I found the toilet next to the tree.

**1**  빈칸 ⓐ와 ⓑ에 공통으로 들어갈 낱말을 쓰세요.

_____

**2**  윗글의 I가 밤중에 깬 이유가 무엇인지 우리말로 쓰세요.

_____

**3**  일이 일어난 순서대로 번호를 쓰세요.

_____    _____    _____    _____

I went in and locked the door. It was quiet. Soon I heard someone's footsteps.

The sound was getting louder and louder.

Then it stopped in front of me. I was really scared.

I thought, "_____©_____ Is it a ghost?

Maybe it is waiting to eat me."

Then I thought, "I'm a brave girl. I can fight the ghost!"

I opened the door with a loud sound to scare the ghost.

Then it screamed and I screamed too.

"AHHHHH!"

Thank God, it was my sister.

She said, "Why would you do that? You scared me!"

---

**4** 빈칸 ©에 가장 어울리는 것을 고르세요.

① Why was the ghost here?

② Why did the ghost meet my family?

③ Why did the sound stop in front of me?

**5** 윗글의 I가 화장실 안에서 들은 소리가 무엇인지 우리말로 쓰세요.

_____

**6** 윗글의 내용과 다른 그림을 고르세요.

①   ②   ③

**31**

## Build up your word power.

⊙ **a few**

몇몇의: some, or a small number of something

_____ months ago, my family had a trip to Canada.

⊙ **drive** 〔과거형: drove〕

운전하다: to move or travel on land in a motor vehicle

Dad _____ very long hours.

⊙ **campsite**

캠프장: a piece of land where people on holiday can camp

We set up the tent at the _____.

⊙ **wake up** 〔과거형: woke up〕

잠이 깨다: to become awake and conscious after sleeping

I _____ in the middle of the night.

⊙ **dark**

어두운: with little or no light

It was _____.

⊙ **look for** 〔과거형: looked for〕

…을 찾다: to try to find a particular thing or person

I went out and _____ the toilet.

32

⊙ **lock** 〔과거형: locked〕

잠그다: to fasten something so that other people cannot open it

I _____ the door.

⊙ **footstep** 〔복수형: footsteps〕

발소리: the sound of each step when someone is walking

I heard someone's _____.

⊙ **ghost**

유령: the spirit of a dead person

Is it a _____?

⊙ **brave**

용감한: showing no fear of dangerous or difficult things

I'm a _____ girl.

⊙ **fight**

싸우다: to use physical force to defeat someone or something

I can _____ the ghost.

⊙ **scream** 〔과거형: screamed〕

소리치다: to cry or say something loudly

I _____.

**1  Choose the correct word for the blank.**

> I'm sad _____ my friend moved away.

ⓐ why          ⓑ what          ⓒ because

**2  Choose the correct sentence for the blank.**

> *A:* _____
>
> *B:* Because she is busy.

ⓐ Who is Ann?

ⓑ Why can't Ann go with us?

ⓒ Why did Ann make a cake?

**3  Read the dialog and write the answer to the question.**

> *Ms. Pitt:* Gary, you are late.
>
> *Gary:*    I'm sorry, Ms. Pitt.
>          I went to bed at 2 o'clock in the morning,
>          so I got up late.
>
> *Ms. Pitt:* Oh, boy!

*Q:* Why is Gary late?

*A:* _____

**4** Choose the correct expression for the blank.

> I'm cooking dinner _____.
> It's my first time making spaghetti. They'll be very happy.

ⓐ because I don't like spaghetti

ⓑ because my parents will eat out

ⓒ because I want to surprise my parents

[5~6] Read and answer the questions.

> *Susan:* Welcome to my house!
> *Betsy:* Thank you for inviting me. Can I look around?
> *Susan:* Sure. I'll show you around. Follow me.
>  This is the living room.
> *Betsy:* Oh! _____ ⓐ _____
> *Susan:* Because everyone in my family loves that chair.
>  So we decided to put it in the middle of the room.
> *Betsy:* That's unusual.

**5** Which of the following is the best expression in ____ ⓐ ____ ?

ⓐ Why is the chair broken?

ⓑ Why is the chair upside down?

ⓒ Why is the chair in the middle of the room?

**6** Which of the following is suitable for the blank?

Susan's family loves _____ , so they put it in the middle of the room.

ⓐ the chair            ⓑ the living room            ⓒ the plant

**Would You Like to Come?**

**Listen and repeat the dialog.** T12

 We're having a surprise party for my brother today. Would you like to come?

 Yes, I'd love to.

 Come to my house by 5 o'clock.

 Okay. See you then.

**Speak aloud.** T13

**1**

go to the movies

**2**

play outside

**3**

eat something

## Listen and choose the correct picture.  T14

1 ⓐ 　　ⓑ 　　ⓒ

2 ⓐ 　　ⓑ 　　ⓒ

## Listen and choose the correct dialog for the picture. ⊙ T15

## Listen and choose the correct dialog. ⊙ T16

## Listen and repeat the words. T17

play outside

make a reservation

order

come along

look at

eat something

## Listen and write the number. T18

_____    _____    _____

**Circle the correct word for the picture.**

1

order

eat something

2

make a reservation

look at

3

come along

play outside

4

play outside

make a reservation

**Unscramble the letters and complete the sentence.**

1

Would you like to _____?

d e r o r

2

Would you like to _____ _____?

a t e t n i g s m h o e

**What are they saying? Choose the correct sentence.**

1

    ⓐ Would you like to play outside?

    ⓑ Would you like to look at the ball?

    ⓒ Would you like to come to my house?

2

    ⓐ Would you like to order?

    ⓑ Would you like to come along?

    ⓒ Would you like to make a reservation?

3

    ⓐ Would you like to come along?

    ⓑ Would you like to play outside?

    ⓒ Would you like to eat something?

**Match the pairs to make a dialog.**

 Would you like to come?

 Okay. See you then.

 Come to my house by 3 o'clock.

 Yes, I'd love to.

 CHALLENGE!

**Choose the correct answer for the blank.**

1
> *A:* Jenny, _____?
>
> *B:* No, thank you. I'm not hungry.

ⓐ what would you like to do

ⓑ would you like to play outside

ⓒ would you like to eat something

2
> *Annie:* Jason, would you like to go hiking?
>
> *Jason:* Yes, I'd love to. I like hiking very much.
>
> But I'm tired. I would like to stay at home now.
>
> *Annie:* I see. Well, how about next Saturday?
>
> *Jason:* Okay.

Jason wants to _____ but he is going to _____ now.

ⓐ go hiking – stay at home

ⓑ stay at home – go hiking

ⓒ go hiking – climb a mountain

3
> *A:* Would you like to make a reservation?
>
> *B:* Yes. I want a single room for two nights from tomorrow.
>
> *A:* What's your name, sir?
>
> *B:* My name's Billy Watson.
>
> *A:* Okay.

Where does Mr. Watson call to make a reservation?

ⓐ A hotel.          ⓑ A theater.          ⓒ A restaurant.

## Choose and write the correct word for the picture.

| look at | come along | eat something | play outside |

**1**

_____

**2**

_____

**3**

_____

**4**

_____

## Fill in the blank and complete the dialog.

**1**

*A:* Would you like to _____?
*B:* Yes, please.

**2**

*A:* _____ you like to come along?
*B:* No, thanks. I'm tired.

**3**

*A:* Would you _____?
*B:* Yes, I'd love to.

## Unscramble and write the question.

**1**

A: _____ ?

( would / like to / you / a reservation / make )

B: Yes, please.

**2**

A: _____ ?

( like to / play / you / would / outside )

B: I'm sorry, but I'm tired.

## Number the sentences in order and write them.

_____ Yes, I'd love to.

__1__ I'm having my birthday party.

_____ Okay. See you then.

_____ Come to my house by 5 o'clock tomorrow.

_____ Would you like to come?

 I'm having my birthday party. _____

_____

# Bully Billy's Trick

**Choose and complete the cartoon.**

| I'm not hungry. | come along |
| eat something | Would you like to order? |

[1~4] Listen and write the number. T19

[5~6] Listen and choose the correct picture. T20

5 ⓐ  ⓑ  ⓒ

6 ⓐ  ⓑ  ⓒ

[7~8] Choose the correct word for the blank.

7  *A:* _____ you like to play outside?
   *B:* Yes, I'd love to.

   ⓐ What              ⓑ Would              ⓒ Who

8  *A:* Would you _____ a reservation?
   *B:* Yes, please.

   ⓐ want making       ⓑ want to make       ⓒ like to make

[9~10] Read the dialog and answer the questions.

> *Jill:*  Hi, Sam. How are you?
> *Sam:* Hi, Jill. I'm great. I'm going to the movies now.
> _____ⓐ_____
> *Jill:*  Yes, I'd love to. What movie are you going to see?
> *Sam:* I don't know yet. Let's go and see.
> *Jill:*  Okay.

9  Which of the following is the best expression in _____ⓐ_____ ?

   ⓐ Would you like to order?
   ⓑ Would you like to play outside?
   ⓒ Would you like to come along?

10 Which of the following is NOT true about the dialog?

   ⓐ Sam feels great.
   ⓑ Sam is going to see "Finding Nemo Ⅱ".
   ⓒ Sam and Jill are going to the movies.

# Would You Help Me, Please?

**Quiz**

A: _____ you help me, please?

B: Sure.

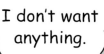

**Quiz**

Q: What would the man like to do?

A: He _____ _____ to have _____ .

## ■ would like to do

…하고 싶다(= want to do)라는 뜻의 관용 표현으로 to 다음에는 동사원형이 쓰인다.

---

*A:* Would you like to play outside?    너, 나가서 놀고 싶니?
*B:* No, I'm tired.    아니, 나 피곤해.
*A:* Then what would you like to do?    그럼 뭐 하고 싶은데?
*B:* I would (I'd) like to go to bed.    나 자고 싶어.

---

| I<br>You<br>He<br>We<br>They | would like | to go swimming. |
|---|---|---|

## Fill in the blanks and complete the dialog.

**1** *A:* What _____ you like to do?

    *B:* I _____ like to play outside.

**2** *A:* _____ would you like to do?

    *B:* I _____ like to have dinner.

**3** *A:* _____ you like to make a reservation?

    *B:* Yes, I _____ love to.

**4** *A:* Would you _____ to try this pie?

    *B:* _____, thanks. I'm full.

**Change the sentence using 'would like to do'.**

**1** I want to look at the menu.

_____

**2** We want to eat something.

_____

**3** Do you want to go swimming?

_____

**4** What do you want to do?

_____

**Unscramble the words to complete the dialog.**

**1** | like | you | to do | what | would | ? |

_A:_ _____

_B:_ I'd like to go camping.

**2** | to order | would | like | you | ? |

_A:_ _____

_B:_ Yes, please.

**3** | I'd | a reservation | like | to make | . |

_A:_ What would you like to do?

_B:_ _____

# ■ Modal Verb: Would

조동사 would를 사용하여 공손한 부탁을 할 수 있다. 'Would＋주어＋동사원형～?'의 형태로 쓰인다.

| | |
|---|---|
| Would you open the door, please? | 문 좀 열어 주시겠어요? |
| Would you tell me the time? | 몇 시인지 알려 주시겠어요? |

## Fill in the blanks and choose the correct response.

| | |
|---|---|
| Sure. | I'm sorry, but I can't. |
| Sure, it's ten thirty. | I'm sorry, but I have to work. |

**1**

A: _____ you close the window?

B: _____

**2**

A: _____ you tell me the time?

B: _____

**3**

A: _____ you play with me?

B: _____

**4**

A: _____ you help me?

B: _____

**Complete the sentence using the given expression and 'would'.**

1 take out the garbage

_____?

2 close the door

_____?

3 read a book to me

_____?

**Unscramble and write the sentence.**

1 | you | would | the window | open | ? |

_____

2 | me | you | help | would | ? |

_____

3 | would | check | my report | you | ? |

_____

4 | the time | would | you | me | tell | ? |

_____

53

# The Fox and the Crane 🔘 T21

One day, a Fox called a Crane and invited him to dinner.

🦊 Would you ____ⓐ____ have dinner with me?

🐦 Sure.

When the Crane went to the Fox's home, he saw
two plates of bean soup on the table.
The soup smelled good.
"Help yourself," said the Fox.
The Crane tried to eat the soup, but it fell out
of his beak.

---

**1** 빈칸 ⓐ에 알맞은 말을 쓰세요.

_____

**2** 학이 왜 스프를 먹지 못했는지 우리말로 쓰세요.

_____

**3** 다음 중 윗글의 내용과 다른 그림을 고르세요.

① 　② 　③

He couldn't eat any soup. The Fox laughed at him.

A few days later, the Crane called the Fox.

 _____ⓑ_____ you like to come to my house tonight?

 Sure.

When the Fox went to the Crane's home,
the food smelled great. The Crane put two bottles
on the table. The Fox tried to eat the food,
but he couldn't eat any food in the bottle.

**4** 빈칸 ⓑ에 알맞은 말을 쓰세요. _____

**5** 일이 일어난 순서대로 번호를 쓰세요.

_____   _____   _____   _____

**6** 윗글의 내용과 어울리는 속담을 고르세요.

① No pain, No gain.

② Many drops make a shower.

③ Do to others as you would be done by them.

# Build up your word power.

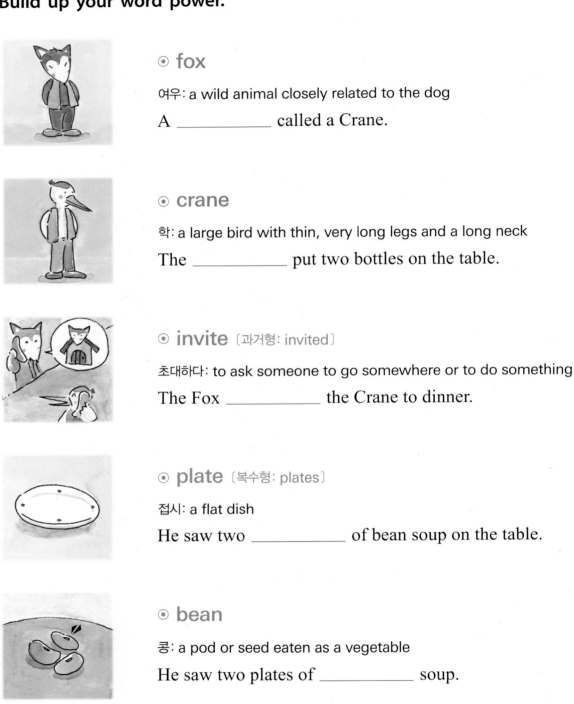

⊙ **fox**

여우: a wild animal closely related to the dog

A _____ called a Crane.

⊙ **crane**

학: a large bird with thin, very long legs and a long neck

The _____ put two bottles on the table.

⊙ **invite** 〔과거형: invited〕

초대하다: to ask someone to go somewhere or to do something

The Fox _____ the Crane to dinner.

⊙ **plate** 〔복수형: plates〕

접시: a flat dish

He saw two _____ of bean soup on the table.

⊙ **bean**

콩: a pod or seed eaten as a vegetable

He saw two plates of _____ soup.

⊙ **smell** 〔과거형: smelled〕

냄새가 나다: to give off specified odor

The soup _____ good.

◉ **try** 〔과거형: tried〕

노력하다: to make an effort to do something

The Crane _____ to eat the soup.

◉ **tonight**

오늘 밤: the night of today

Would you like to come to my house _____?

◉ **beak**

부리: the hard, projecting mouth of a bird

The soup fell out of his _____.

◉ **laugh at** 〔과거형: laughed at〕

비웃다: to make unkind or funny remarks about someone
because he〔she〕does or says something stupid

The Fox _____ him.

◉ **bottle** 〔복수형: bottles〕

병: a container to hold liquids

He couldn't eat any food in the _____.

◉ **food**

음식: something people and animals eat

The Fox tried to eat the _____.

**1** Choose the correct word for the blanks.

> _____ you open the door, please?
> Tom _____ like to dance.

    ⓐ What〔what〕         ⓑ Would〔would〕         ⓒ Is〔is〕

**2** Choose the correct sentence for the blank.

> *A:* _____
> *B:* Yes, I'd love to.

    ⓐ Do you love me?

    ⓑ What would you like to do?

    ⓒ Would you like to come along?

**3** Choose the wrong part of the sentences.

> Would you like to come to my house? I'm having a party tomorrow.
>   ⓐ
> Mom would likes to invite all of my friends. Would you like to come?
>        ⓑ                             ⓒ

**4** What's the boy saying? Choose the correct answer.

    ⓐ Would you help me?

    ⓑ Would you play outside?

    ⓒ Would you like to go swimming?

**5** Which of the following is NOT true about the dialog?

> *Jane:* What would you like to do tomorrow?
>
> *Tim:* I'd like to go swimming. What about you, Mike?
>
> *Mike:* I'd like to stay at home.
> Jane, do you also want to go swimming?
>
> *Jane:* Not really. I'd like to go hiking.

ⓐ Mike – go swimming     ⓑ Tim – go swimming     ⓒ Jane – go hiking

[6~7] Read the dialog and answer the questions.

> Annie and Paul are talking about their dreams.
>
> *Paul:* What would you like to do when you grow up?
>
> *Annie:* _____ⓐ_____ become a cook.
>
> *Paul:* Oh, really? Do you like cooking?
>
> *Annie:* Yes, I do. I'd like to cook something new.
>
> *Paul:* That sounds interesting.
>
> *Annie:* How about you, Paul?
>
> *Paul:* I want to become a pilot.
>
> *Annie:* That sounds good, too.

**6** Which of the following is suitable for the blank _____ⓐ_____?

ⓐ I'd like to     ⓑ She'd like to     ⓒ They'd like to

**7** Which of the following is suitable for the blank?

Annie wants to be _____ and Paul wants to be a pilot.

ⓐ a teacher     ⓑ a doctor     ⓒ a cook

# Roller Coaster
**Student Book**

**P. 13**

1
A: Kelly, are you OK? You look sick.
B: I have a headache.

ⓑ

2
A: Why are you so busy?
B: Because I have to finish my homework.

ⓐ

1
ⓐ I have to finish this math homework.
ⓑ I have a toothache.
ⓒ Thank you.

ⓑ

2
ⓐ How are you today?
ⓑ Who is so busy?
ⓒ Why are you so busy?

ⓒ

ⓐ A: Why are you so busy?
   B: I'm very busy.
ⓑ A: Are you OK?
   B: Because I have a cold.
ⓒ A: Why are you so busy?
   B: Because I have to finish my homework.

ⓒ

**P. 14**

1 ⓐ I have a cold.    ⓑ I have an earache.

ⓐ

2 ⓐ I have a toothache.    ⓑ I have a backache.

ⓑ

**P. 15**

1 headache   2 earache   3 backache   4 stomachache

1 I have a cold.    2 I have a headache.
3 I have a stomachache.    4 I have a toothache.

**P. 16**

1 Wendy    2 Tony    3 Brian    4 Julia

1 Are you OK? You look sick.    Because I have to finish this work.

2 Why are you so busy?    I have a toothache.

**P. 17**

1 ⓒ         2 ⓒ

Andy didn't do his homework yesterday because he had a headache.

**P. 18**

1 I have an earache.    2 I have a stomachache.
3 I have a backache.    4 I have a headache.

Are you OK? You look sick.

I have a stomachache.

**P. 19**

2 I have a headache.
3 Then why are you so busy?
4 Because I have to finish this math homework.
5 Oh, my! You should take a rest.

1 Why are you so busy?
2 Because I have to finish my homework.

**P. 20~21**

Why are you so busy?
I have a headache.
Go to bed.

I'm sorry, Mr. Smith. I didn't finish my homework.

**P. 22~23**

<u>2</u>　<u>1</u>　<u>5</u>　<u>3</u>　<u>4</u>

> 🎧 1 I have an earache.
> 2 I have a cold.
> 3 I have a stomachache.
> 4 I have a backache.
> 5 I have a toothache.

6 🎧 ⓐ A: How are you?　B: I have a backache.
> ⓑ A: Why are you so busy?
> 　B: I have a headache.
> ⓒ A: Are you OK?　B: No, I have a headache.

ⓒ

7 🎧 ⓐ A: Why are you so busy?
> 　B: Because I have to finish this homework.
> ⓑ A: Are you OK?　B: I have a cold.
> ⓒ A: How is it?　B: It's great.

ⓐ

8 <u>ⓑ</u> I have an earache.
9 <u>ⓒ</u> I have a toothache.
10 <u>ⓐ</u> I have a stomachache.
11 ⓒ
**/해석/** 애니: 왜 그렇게 바쁘니?
　　조앤: 해야 할 일이 많거든.
　　애니: 어떤 거?
　　조앤: 수학 숙제, 영어 숙제, 과학 숙제가 있어.
12 ⓑ
**/해석/** 마이크: 왜 샘은 여기에 없니?
　　소냐: 왜냐하면 독감에 걸렸거든.
　　마이크: 오, 안됐다. 샘은 파티에 못 가겠네.

**UNIT 02**

**P. 24~25**

Q: Why is the alien in the garden?
A: Maybe it wants to be the girls' friend.

Q: Why did the boy come to the girls' house?
A: Because he wants to scare them.

**P. 26**

1 A: Why are you so happy?
2 A: Why can't you play soccer?
3 A: Why did Eric make a cake?
4 A: Why doesn't Sue want a doll?

**P. 27**

1 Why are they so excited?
2 Why didn't you study hard yesterday?
3 Why wasn't she happy about the party?

1 A: Why are you late?
2 A: Why are you all wet?
3 A: Why did Jake buy that jacket?
4 A: Why was Kim so sad?

**P. 28**

1 Jasmine came home early because she was sick.
　ⓐ

2 B: Because I had a test yesterday.
　ⓐ

**P. 29**

1 I don't eat pizza because I'm on a diet.
2 I didn't hear the noise because I fell asleep.
3 I'm cooking dinner because I want to surprise my parents.

1 B: Because he had to walk the dog.
2 B: Because we didn't clean after the party.
3 I need a new bag because my bag is old.
4 Sandy isn't sleepy because she took a long nap.

**P. 30~31**

1 because
2 화장실에 가기 위해서
3

<u>3</u>　　<u>1</u>　　<u>4</u>　　<u>2</u>

4 ③
5 누군가의[언니의] 발소리
6 ③

/ 해석 / 캠프장의 유령

몇 달 전, 나의 가족은 캐나다로 여행을 갔다. 아빠가 오랜 시간 운전하셨다. 점점 어두워졌고, 우리는 캠프장을 찾아서 텐트를 쳤다. 우리는 함께 저녁을 먹고 잠자리에 들었다. 우리는 아침에 일찍 떠나야 했기 때문에 일찍 자야만 했다.

나는 화장실에 가야 해서 한밤중에 잠이 깼다. 어두웠고 화장실에 가기 무서웠지만, 나는 식구들을 깨우고 싶지 않았다.

그래서 나는 밖으로 나와서 화장실을 찾았다. 전등이 켜져 있어서 그렇게 무섭지는 않았다. 나는 나무 옆에서 화장실을 찾았다.

나는 들어가서 문을 잠궜다. 조용했지만 나는 곧 누군가의 발소리를 들었다. 그 소리는 점점 커졌다. 그리고 그 소리는 내 앞에서 멈췄다. 나는 정말 무서웠다. "왜 소리가 내 앞에서 멈췄지? 유령인가? 아마 나를 잡아먹으려고 기다리는 걸 거야."라고 생각했다. 그러자, "나는 용감한 소녀야. 유령과 싸울 수 있어!"라는 생각이 들었다.

나는 유령을 겁주기 위해 요란하게 문을 열었다. 그러자 유령이 비명을 질렀고 나도 역시 비명을 질렀다. "아~~~~~~~!"

세상에, 그건 나의 언니였다. 언니가 말했다, "왜 그랬어? 너 때문에 놀랐잖아!"


P. 32~33

A few **months** ago, my family had a trip to Canada.
Dad **drove** very long hours.
We set up the tent at the **campsite**.
I **woke up** in the middle of the night.
It was **dark**.
I went out and **looked for** the toilet.

I **locked** the door.
I heard someone's **footsteps**.
Is it a **ghost**?
I'm a **brave** girl.
I can **fight** the ghost.
I **screamed**.


P. 34~35

1 ⓒ        2 ⓑ
3 Because he got up late.
4 ⓒ
/ 해석 / 나는 부모님을 놀라게 해 드리려고 저녁을 짓고 있다.
스파게티를 만드는 것은 이번이 처음이다.
부모님이 매우 좋아하실 것이다.
5 ⓒ        6 ⓐ
/ 해석 / 수잔: 우리 집에 온 걸 환영해!
벳시: 초대해 줘서 고마워. 둘러봐도 될까?

---

수잔: 물론이지. 내가 구경시켜 줄게. 따라와. 여긴 거실이야.
벳시: 어! 왜 의자가 방 한 가운데 있니?
수잔: 왜냐하면 우리 가족 모두 저 의자를 좋아하거든.
      그래서 방 가운데 놓기로 결정했어.
벳시: 흔한 일은 아니네.


## UNIT 03

P. 37

1
A: Would you like to come?
B: Yes, I'd love to.

ⓒ

2
A: Would you like to eat something?
B: No, thank you. I'm full.

ⓑ

ⓐ A: What are you doing?
   B: I'm eating now.
ⓑ A: What's wrong?
   B: I have a stomachache.
ⓒ A: Would you like to play outside?
   B: Yes, I'd love to.

ⓒ

ⓐ A: Would you like to come?
   B: I'm sorry, but I can't.
ⓑ A: Would you like to eat something?
   B: I don't like pizza.
ⓒ A: Why are you so busy?
   B: Yes, I'd love to.

ⓐ

P. 38

_3_        _2_        _1_

1. order    2. look at    3. make a reservation

**P. 39**

1  order                         2  look at
3  come along                    4  play outside

1  Would you like to order?
2  Would you like to eat something?

**P. 40**

1 ⓐ              2 ⓐ              3 ⓒ

Would you like to come?  ✕  Okay. See you then.
Come to my house by 3 o'clock.  Yes, I'd love to.

**P. 41**

1 ⓒ              2 ⓐ              3 ⓐ

**P. 42**

1  look at                       2  play outside
3  eat something                 4  come along

1  A: Would you like to order?
2  A: Would you like to come along?
3  A: Would you like to play outside?

**P. 43**

1  A: Would you like to make a reservation?
2  A: Would you like to play outside?

_3_  Yes, I'd love to.
_1_  I'm having my birthday party.
_5_  Okay. See you then.
_4_  Come to my house by 5 o'clock tomorrow.
_2_  Would you like to come?

I'm having my birthday party.
Would you like to come?
Yes, I'd love to.
Come to my house by 5 o'clock tomorrow.
Okay. See you then.

**P. 44~45**

Would you like to come along?
Would you like to eat something?

Would you like to order?
Whoops! I'm not hungry. Give it to him, please.

**P. 46~47**

 2    3    1    4

1  look at              2  make a reservation
3  play outside         4  eat something

5
A: Would you like to order?
B: Yes, please.

ⓐ

6
A: Would you like to come along?
B: No, thanks. I'm tired.

ⓑ
7 ⓑ              8 ⓒ
9        ⓒ        10        ⓑ

**/해석 /**  질: 안녕, 샘. 잘 지내니?
샘: 안녕, 질. 잘 지내. 나 지금 영화 보러 가는 길이야. 같이 갈래?
질: 좋아. 어떤 영화 보러 가는데?
샘: 아직 모르겠어. 가서 알아보자.
질: 좋아.

**UNIT 04**

**P. 48~49**

Q: Would you help me, please?
A: Sure.

Q: What would the man like to do?
A: He would like to have dinner.

**P. 50**

1  A: What would you like to do?
   B: I would like to play outside.

2 *A:* What would you like to do?
  *B:* I would like to have dinner.
3 *A:* Would you like to make a reservation?
  *B:* Yes, I would love to.
4 *A:* Would you like to try this pie?
  *B:* No, thanks. I'm full.

## P. 51

1 I would like to look at the menu.
2 We would like to eat something.
3 Would you like to go swimming?
4 What would you like to do?

1 *A:* What would you like to do?
2 *A:* Would you like to order?
3 *B:* I'd like to make a reservation.

## P. 52

1 *A:* Would you close the window?
  *B:* Sure.
2 *A:* Would you tell me the time?
  *B:* Sure, it's ten thirty.
3 *A:* Would you play with me?
  *B:* I'm sorry, but I have to work.
4 *A:* Would you help me?
  *B:* I'm sorry, but I can't.

## P. 53

1 Would you take out the garbage?
2 Would you close the door?
3 Would you read a book to me?

1 Would you open the window?
2 Would you help me?
3 Would you check my report?
4 Would you tell me the time?

## P. 54~55

1 like to    2 수프가 부리에서 흘러서    3 ①    4 would
5
 4    2    1    3

6 ③

**/ 해석 /**  학

어느 날, 여우가 학에게 전화를 해서 그를 저녁 식사에 초대했다.

"나와 함께 저녁 먹을래?"  "좋아."

학이 여우의 집에 갔을 때, 학은 식탁 위에 있는 콩 수프 두 접시를 보았다. 그 수프는 냄새가 좋았다. "마음껏 먹어," 여우가 말했다.

학은 수프를 먹으려고 노력했지만, 수프가 부리 밖으로 흘러내렸다. 그는 수프를 하나도 먹지 못했다. 여우는 학을 비웃었다.

며칠 후, 학이 여우에게 전화를 했다.

"오늘 밤 우리 집에 올래?"  "좋아."

여우가 학의 집에 갔을 때, 좋은 음식 냄새가 났다. 학은 식탁 위에 병 두 개를 놓았다. 여우는 음식을 먹으려고 노력했지만, 병 안에 든 음식을 하나도 먹지 못했다.

## P. 56~57

A Fox called a Crane.
The Crane put two bottles on the table.
The Fox invited the Crane to dinner.
He saw two plates of bean soup on the table.
He saw two plates of bean soup.
The soup smelled good.

The Crane tried to eat the soup.
Would you like to come to my house tonight?
The soup fell out of his beak.
The Fox laughed at him.
He couldn't eat any food in the bottle.
The Fox tried to eat the food.

## P. 58~59

1 ⓑ        2 ⓒ        3 ⓑ        4 ⓐ
5 ⓐ        6 ⓐ        7 ⓒ

**/ 해석 /**  애니와 폴이 그들의 장래 희망에 대해서 이야기하고 있다.
    폴:  너 이 다음에 크면 무엇을 하고 싶니?
    *애니:* 나는 요리사가 되고 싶어.
    폴:  와, 정말? 너 요리하는 거 좋아해?
    *애니:* 응, 좋아해. 나는 뭔가 새로운 걸 요리하는 게 좋아.
    폴:  그거 재미있겠다.
    *애니:* 너는 어때, 폴?
    폴:  나는 비행기 조종사가 되고 싶어.
    *애니:* 그것도 역시 좋은 생각이야.

# Roller Coaster
## Workbook & Test

**UNIT 01**

**P. 2**

B

| s | d | t | d | s | e | h | f | m | u | d |
|---|---|---|---|---|---|---|---|---|---|---|
| g | t | o | h | e | o | e | s | g | o | w |
| l | a | o | h | c | n | a | e | s | k | x |
| b | z | t | m | r | y | d | h | w | i | b |
| n | t | h | e | a | r | a | c | h | e | a |
| a | c | a | d | r | c | c | b | s | u | c |
| i | x | c | k | q | e | h | c | l | f | k |
| c | r | h | p | l | d | e | a | f | e | a |
| l | o | e | f | j | d | b | g | c | i | c |
| p | m | l | c | s | x | r | j | u | h | h |
| d | k | r | d | c | e | q | o | x | a | e |

1 headache　　　　　2 cold
3 earache　　　　　4 toothache
5 stomachache　　　6 backache

**P. 5**

D

1 cold　　　　　　2 headache
3 earache　　　　　4 toothache
5 backache　　　　6 stomachache

E

I　Why are you so ①busy?
　②Because I have to finish this homework.
II　Are you OK? You look ③sick.
　I have a ④cold.
　Oh, my! You should ⑤take a rest.

**UNIT 02**

**P. 7**

B

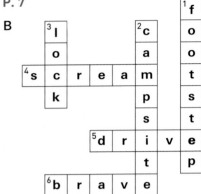

1 footstep　　　　　2 campsite
3 lock　　　　　　4 scream
5 drive　　　　　　6 brave

**P. 8**

C

1 Why　　2 Why　　3 Why

D

1 Why are they excited?
2 Why did you make a cake?
3 Why can't you play soccer?

**P. 9**

E

1 Because　2 because　3 because

F

1 Because she is hungry.
2 Because I want to surprise my parents.
3 Jasmine came home early because she was sick.

**P. 10**

G

1 drive　　　　　　2 dark
3 scream　　　　　4 footstep
5 ghost　　　　　　6 lock

**H**

1 Why did you make a cake?

2 Because it's Mom's birthday.

3 A few months ago, my family had a trip to Canada.

4 I went out and looked for the toilet.

5 Why did the sound stop in front of me?

UNIT 03

P. 12

**B**

1 play outside

2 eat something

3 look at

4 make a reservation

5 order

6 come along

P. 15

**D**

1 eat something

2 order

3 look at

4 make a reservation

5 play outside

6 come along

**E**

Ⅰ Hi, Clara. It's my brother's birthday tomorrow.

  ①Would you like to come?

  Yes, I'd ②love to.

  Come to my house at 3 o'clock.

  See you ③then.

Ⅱ I'd like to ④make a reservation.

  ⑤When will you come?

  Tomorrow night at seven.

  Okay.

UNIT 04

P. 17

**B**

| i | w | o | n | t | p | e | a | s | l |
|---|---|---|---|---|---|---|---|---|---|
| q | t | r | s | o | f | j | k | m | c |
| y | g | t | i | n | v | i | t | e | e |
| a | u | u | y | q | n | m | r | l | g |
| p | l | a | t | e | j | k | y | l | h |
| v | b | e | a | k | o | k | p | k | i |
| b | o | t | t | l | e | r | e | o | f |
| k | q | w | g | c | r | a | n | e | o |
| t | o | n | i | g | h | t | p | y | x |

| | |
|---|---|
| 1 invite | 2 beak |
| 3 plate | 4 fox |
| 5 smell | 6 crane |
| 7 tonight | 8 bottle |

P. 18

**C**

1 Would    2 Would    3 Would

**D**

1 Would you take out the garbage?

2 Would you go outside with me?

3 Would you tell me the time?

P. 19

**E**

1 What would you like to do?

2 Would you like to go swimming?

3 Would you like to try this pie?

**F**

1 I would like to eat something.

2 I would like to have dinner.

3 I'd like to go camping.

**P. 20**

**G**

1 bean      2 bottle

3 plate      4 beak

5 crane      6 laugh at

**H**

1 Would you tell me the time?

2 Sure, it's two ten.

3 A fox called a crane and invited him to dinner.

4 The soup fell out of his beak.

5 A few days later, the crane called the fox.

6 The fox tried to eat the food.

**Achievement Test**

1 🎧 have a headache

ⓐ

2 🎧 have a toothache

ⓒ

3 🎧 ⓐ A: Are you OK?   B: I have a toothache.
     ⓑ A: You look sick.   B: Yes, I have an earache.
     ⓒ A: Are you OK?   B: Because I have a cold.

ⓐ

4 🎧 ⓐ A: Why are you busy?
       B: Yes, I'm very busy.
     ⓑ A: Are you OK?
       B: I have a cold.
     ⓒ A: Why are you so busy?
       B: Because I'm doing my homework.

ⓒ

5 ⓑ          6 ⓑ

7 ⓐ          8 ⓒ

9 ⓑ

10 I have a cold because I didn't wear a coat.

11 ⓒ

12 because Joseph had a headache

**Final Test**

1 🎧 ⓐ look at
     ⓑ order
     ⓒ eat something

ⓐ

2 🎧 ⓐ make a reservation
     ⓑ come along
     ⓒ play outside

ⓒ

3 🎧 Q: Would you like to make a reservation?
     ⓐ No, thanks.
     ⓑ Yes, please.
     ⓒ Okay, see you then.

ⓑ

4 🎧 ⓐ A: Would you like to eat something?
       B: No, thanks.
     ⓑ A: Would you like to come along?
       B: No, thanks.
     ⓒ A: Would you like to come along?
       B: Yes, I'd love to.

ⓑ

5 ⓑ          6 ⓒ

7 ⓐ          8 ⓑ

9 ⓒ          10 ⓐ

11 Because she is busy with her homework.

12 ⓐ

# 01 I Have a Cold

## A Write and say aloud.

1  머리가 아프다        have a headache

2  이가 아프다          have a toothache

3  귀가 아프다          have an earache

4  배가 아프다          have a stomachache

5  감기에 걸리다        have a cold

6  허리가 아프다        have a backache

7  왜 (의문사)          why

8  왜냐하면 (접속사)     because

9  바쁜                busy

10  아픈               sick

11  마치다             finish

12  쉬다               take a rest

## B Circle and write the word.

| s | d | t | d | s | e | h | f | m | u | d |
|---|---|---|---|---|---|---|---|---|---|---|
| g | t | o | h | e | o | e | s | g | o | w |
| l | a | o | h | c | n | a | e | s | k | x |
| b | z | t | m | r | y | d | h | w | i | b |
| n | t | h | e | a | r | a | c | h | e | a |
| a | c | a | d | r | c | c | b | s | u | c |
| i | x | c | k | q | e | h | c | l | f | k |
| c | r | h | o | l | d | e | a | f | e | a |
| l | o | e | f | j | d | b | g | c | i | c |
| p | m | l | c | s | x | r | j | u | h | h |
| d | k | r | d | c | e | q | o | x | a | e |

1 두통 _____

2 감기 _____

3 귀앓이 _____

4 치통 _____

5 복통 _____

6 요통 _____

## C Write and say aloud.

1 괜찮니? 아파 보여.

Are you OK? You look sick.

2 (나는) 감기에 걸렸어.

I have a cold.

3 (나는) 이가 아파.

I have a toothache.

4 (나는) 머리가 아파.

I have a headache.

5 (나는) 배가 아파.

I have a stomachache.

**6** (나는) 귀가 아파.

I have an earache.

**7** (나는) 허리가 아파.

I have a backache.

**8** 너는 왜 그렇게 바쁘니?

Why are you so busy?

**9** 왜냐하면 나는 이 수학 숙제를 끝내야 하기 때문이야.

Because I have to finish this math homework.

**10** 너는 쉬어야 해.

You should take a rest.

## D Listen and write the word. 🎧 💿 T22

1 _____

2 _____

3 _____

4 _____

5 _____

6 _____

## E Listen and fill in the blanks. 🎧 💿 T23

I　Why are you so ① _____?

　　② _____ I have to _____ this homework.

II　Are you OK? You look ③ _____.

　　I have a ④ _____.

　　Oh, my! You should ⑤ _____.

# 02 Why Is the Alien in Our Garden?

## A Write and say aloud.

| 1 | 몇몇의 | a few |
|---|---|---|
| 2 | 운전하다 | drive |
| 3 | 캠프장 | campsite |
| 4 | 어두운 | dark |
| 5 | ~을 찾다 | look for |
| 6 | 잠그다 | lock |
| 7 | 발소리 | footstep |
| 8 | 유령 | ghost |
| 9 | 용감한 | brave |
| 10 | 소리치다 | scream |
| 11 | 싸우다 | fight |
| 12 | 잠이 깨다 | wake up |

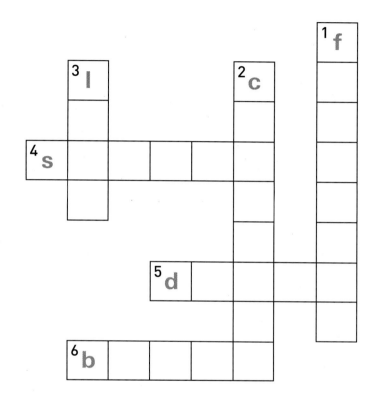

## B Do the crossword puzzle and write the words.

1 발소리 _____

2 캠프장 _____

3 잠그다 _____

4 소리치다 _____

5 운전하다 _____

6 용감한 _____

Fill in the blank.

1 왜 내가 거기에 갔을까?

_____ did I go there? ·

2 왜 앤은 우리와 함께 못 가니?

_____ can't Ann go with us?

3 Jake는 왜 그 재킷을 샀니?

_____ did Jake buy that jacket?

D Unscramble and write the sentence.

1 왜 그들이 신나하니?

| are | why | they | excited |

_____?

2 왜 너는 케이크를 만들었니?

| make | you | did | why | a cake |

_____?

3 왜 너는 축구를 못 하니?

| you | can't | soccer | play | why |

_____?

**E** Fill in the blank.

1 왜냐하면 그는 개를 산책시켜야만 했기 때문이야.

_____ he had to walk the dog.

2 나는 잠이 들어서 그 소음을 듣지 못했어.

I didn't hear the noise _____ I fell asleep.

3 Tom은 운동하는 것을 좋아해서 스포츠 클럽에 가입했어.

Tom joined the sports club _____ he likes to play sports.


**F** Unscramble and write the sentence.

1 왜냐하면 그녀는 배가 고프기 때문이야.

| hungry | because | is | she |

_____ .

2 왜냐하면 나는 부모님을 놀라게 해 드리고 싶거든.

| my parents | I | want | because | to surprise |

_____ .

3 자스민은 아파서 일찍 집에 왔어.

| she | came home | early | Jasmine | because | was sick |

_____ .

**G** Listen and write the word. 🎧 ⊙ T24

1 _____

2 _____

3 _____

4 _____

5 _____

6 _____


**H** Listen and fill in the blanks. 🎧 ⊙ T25

1 _____ did you _____?

2 _____ it's Mom's birthday.

3 _____ months ago, my family had

a _____ to Canada.

4 I went out and _____ the _____.

5 _____ did the sound stop _____ me?

# 03 Would You Like to Come?

**A** **Write and say aloud.**

| | | |
|---|---|---|
| 1 | ~하고 싶다 | would like to |
| 2 | 주문하다 | order |
| 3 | 밖에서 놀다 | play outside |
| 4 | 무엇인가를 먹다 | eat something |
| 5 | 따라오다 | come along |
| 6 | ~을 보다 | look at |
| 7 | 예약하다 | make a reservation |
| 8 | 영화 보러 가다 | go to the movies |
| 9 | 하이킹 하러 가다 | go hiking |
| 10 | 집에 머물다 | stay at home |
| 11 | 깜짝 파티 | surprise party |
| 12 | 내일 | tomorrow |

## B Unscramble and write the word.

1
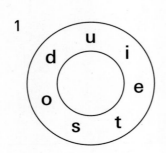

밖에서 놀다

play _____

2
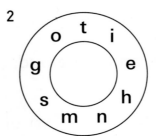

무엇인가를 먹다

eat _____

3
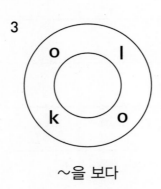

~을 보다

_____ at

4
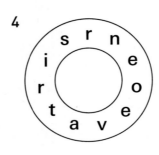

예약하다

make a _____

5
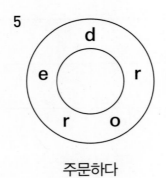

주문하다

_____

6
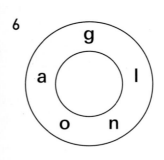

따라오다

come _____

## C Write and say aloud.

1 내 생일 파티를 할 거야.

I'm having my birthday party.


2 우리 집에 올래?

Would you like to come to my house?


3 우리 집에 5시까지 와.

Come to my house by 5 o'clock.


4 영화 보러 갈래?

Would you like to go to the movies?


5 뭐 먹을래?

Would you like to eat something?

6   밖에서 놀래?

Would you like to play outside?

7   그림 보고 싶니?

Would you like to look at the picture?

8   같이 갈래?

Would you like to come along?

9   응, 그러고 싶어.

Yes, I'd love to.

10  고맙지만 괜찮아.

No, thanks.

## D Listen and write the word. 🎧 💿 T26

1 _____

2 _____

3 _____

4 _____

5 _____

6 _____

## E Listen and fill in the blanks. 🎧 💿 T27

I   Hi, Clara. It's my brother's birthday tomorrow.

①_____ you _____ come?

Yes, I'd ②_____ to.

Come to my house at 3 o'clock.

See you ③_____.

II  I'd like to ④_____.

⑤_____ will you come?

Tomorrow night at seven.

Okay.

# 04 Would You Help Me, Please?

## A Write and say aloud.

| | | |
|---|---|---|
| 1 | 여우 | fox |
| 2 | 학 | crane |
| 3 | 초대하다 | invite |
| 4 | 접시 | plate |
| 5 | 콩 | bean |
| 6 | 냄새가 나다 | smell |
| 7 | 노력하다 | try |
| 8 | 부리 | beak |
| 9 | 비웃다 | laugh at |
| 10 | 병 | bottle |
| 11 | 오늘 밤 | tonight |
| 12 | 음식 | food |

## B Circle and write the word.

| i | w | o | n | t | p | e | a | s | l |
|---|---|---|---|---|---|---|---|---|---|
| q | t | r | s | o | f | j | k | m | c |
| y | g | t | i | n | v | i | t | e | e |
| a | u | u | y | q | n | m | r | l | g |
| p | l | a | t | e | j | k | y | l | h |
| v | b | e | a | k | o | k | p | k | i |
| b | o | t | t | l | e | r | e | o | f |
| k | q | w | g | c | r | a | n | e | o |
| t | o | n | i | g | h | t | p | y | x |

1 초대하다 _____

2 부리 _____

3 접시 _____

4 여우 _____

5 냄새가 나다 _____

6 학 _____

7 오늘 밤 _____

8 병 _____

## C Fill in the blank.

1 나 좀 도와줄래?

   _____ you help me?

2 창문 좀 닫아 줄래?

   _____ you close the window?

3 내 보고서 좀 검토해 줄래?

   _____ you check my report?

## D Unscramble and write the sentence.

1 쓰레기 좀 버려 줄래?

   | take out | you | would | the garbage |

   _____?

2 나랑 밖에 좀 같이 가 줄래?

   | you | go outside | would | with me |

   _____?

3 나에게 시간 좀 알려 줄래?

   | the time | would | tell | you | me |

   _____?

18

## E Fill in the blank.

1 뭐 하고 싶니?

What ＿＿＿＿＿＿＿ you ＿＿＿＿＿＿＿ ＿＿＿＿＿＿＿ do?

2 수영하러 가고 싶니?

＿＿＿＿＿＿＿ you ＿＿＿＿＿＿＿ ＿＿＿＿＿＿＿ go swimming?

3 이 파이 먹어 보고 싶니?

＿＿＿＿＿＿＿ you ＿＿＿＿＿＿＿ ＿＿＿＿＿＿＿ try this pie?

## F Unscramble and write the sentence.

1 뭐 좀 먹고 싶어.

| would | to eat | like | something | I |

＿＿＿＿＿＿＿＿＿＿＿＿＿＿＿＿＿＿＿＿＿＿＿＿＿＿ .

2 저녁 먹고 싶어.

| like | dinner | would | to have | I |

＿＿＿＿＿＿＿＿＿＿＿＿＿＿＿＿＿＿＿＿＿＿＿＿＿＿ .

3 캠핑 가고 싶어요.

| like | to go | I'd | camping |

＿＿＿＿＿＿＿＿＿＿＿＿＿＿＿＿＿＿＿＿＿＿＿＿＿＿ .

**G** **Listen and write the word.** 🎧 💿 T28

1 _____

2 _____

3 _____

4 _____

5 _____

6 _____

**H** **Listen and fill in the blanks.** 🎧 💿 T29

1 _____ you tell me the _____?

2 Sure, it's _____.

3 A fox called a _____ and _____ him to dinner.

4 The soup _____ his _____.

5 _____, the crane called the fox.

6 The fox _____ eat the food.